MY TEACHER LIKES TO SAY

By DENISE BRENNAN-NELSON

Illustrated by JANE MONROE DONOVAN

To Nancy Monroe and teachers everywhere
for helping little acorns become mighty oaks.

Denise and Jane

Special thanks to the students and staff at
Hornung Elementary and Southeast Elementary Schools.

Sleeping Bear Press™

310 North Main Street, Suite 300
Chelsea, MI 48118
www.sleepingbearpress.com

© 2006 Sleeping Bear Press is an imprint of Gale, a part of Cengage Learning.

Printed and bound in the United States.

10 9 8 7 6

Library of Congress Cataloging-in-Publication Data

Brennan-Nelson, Denise.
My teacher likes to say / written by Denise Brennan-Nelson;
illustrated by Jane Monroe Donovan.
p. cm.
ISBN 1-58536-212-3
1.English language—Idioms—Juvenile literature. 2.Figures of speech—Juvenile literature.
[1. English language—Idioms. 2. Figures of speech.]I. Monroe Donovan, Jane, ill. II. Title.
PE1462.B745 2004
428.1—dc22   2003025872

Introduction

What comes to mind when you hear the expression, "All eyes on me!"? I used to imagine plucking my eyes out, along with all of my classmates', and putting them on my teacher (yikes)! Of course, she didn't want our eyeballs—she was asking for our attention. And when she would say, "Excuse me, I have a frog in my throat," the whole class would giggle and wonder how it got there. My favorite, though, was when she would say, "I'll be a monkey's uncle!"

These funny and confusing expressions are called maxims, idioms, proverbs, and clichés. There are thousands of them in the English language and they come from many different sources. Some of them are repeated so often they lose their importance, while others provide some of life's most valuable lessons.

If you listen carefully to your teacher, you may hear her using some of these expressions. It's okay if you don't understand them now—you will someday. Until then, have fun using your imagination to picture the special, quirky things your teacher likes to say.

To teachers: In preparing for this book I asked thousands of schoolchildren to tell me what their teacher likes to say. Only **you** can imagine the delightful responses I received! The expressions chosen are not only the things you say, "Put on your thinking cap," but also the philosophy from which you teach, "Great oaks from little acorns grow."

Does your teacher ever say things
that you think are quite amusing?
Does your teacher ever say things
that you find a bit confusing?

My teacher says some funny things
like, "The squeaky wheel gets the oil,"
"Don't beat around the bush,"
and, "A watched pot never boils."

She tells me that I'm "sharp as a tack."
Please tell me what that means!
Sometimes she says I'm "smart as a whip,"
and she thinks I'm "full of beans!"

She often says, "The apple
doesn't fall too far from the tree,"
but I have no idea
what that has to do with me!

My teacher doesn't know this,
but I have a small confession:
I love the things my teacher says—

every sweet and odd expression.

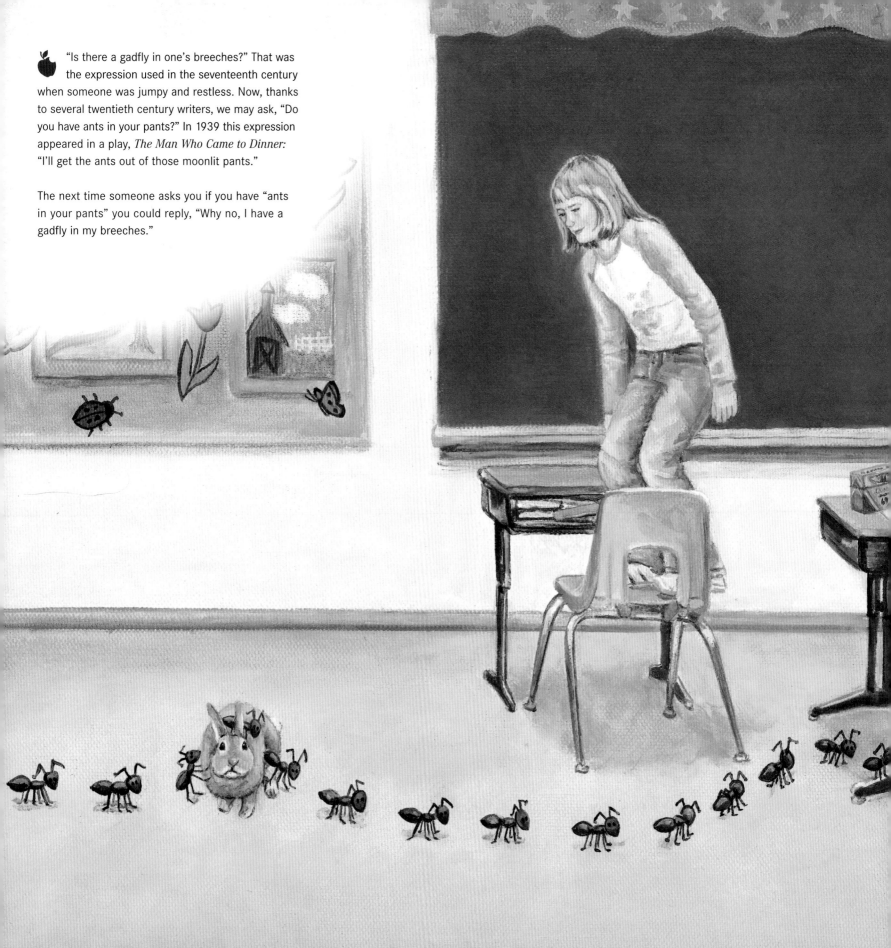

"Is there a gadfly in one's breeches?" That was the expression used in the seventeenth century when someone was jumpy and restless. Now, thanks to several twentieth century writers, we may ask, "Do you have ants in your pants?" In 1939 this expression appeared in a play, *The Man Who Came to Dinner*: "I'll get the ants out of those moonlit pants."

The next time someone asks you if you have "ants in your pants" you could reply, "Why no, I have a gadfly in my breeches."

"Do you have ants in your pants?"

my teacher likes to say.
I'm not sure what she means,
but I like it anyway.

When I have ants in my pants
I squirm and wiggle and shout!
I jump up and down and twist around
'til the ants in my pants fall out!

"Two heads are better than one",

my teacher likes to say.
I'm not sure what she means,
but I like it anyway.

I suppose she's right, a second head
could come in rather handy.
Except for when I have a treat—
which mouth would get the candy?

Have you ever had a hard time figuring something out by yourself? Often when you ask someone to help, you can work it out together.

This expression means that having help from someone else is easier than doing it on your own. It was first used in 1390.

"Put on your thinking cap,"

my teacher likes to say.
I'm not sure what he means,
but I like it anyway.

I wish I had a thinking cap
that did my math for me.
I'd wear it during Science
and at every spelling bee.

Oh no! I think I forgot my thinking cap!

I don't know about you, but I like to daydream. I "put on my thinking cap" when I need to concentrate. When your teacher says this to you, she wants you to focus on what you are doing.

If you had an actual "thinking cap" that could do your thinking for you, what would you want it to think about?

"Please button your lip,"

my teacher likes to say.
I'm not sure what she means,
but I like it anyway.

I'll have to ask my mom to sew
a button on my lip.
Maybe she will add instead
a zipper I could zip.

People may say this to you when they want you to be quiet, or if they tell you a secret that they don't want anyone else to know. This is a twentieth century American expression. Similar expressions are "clam up" and "hold your tongue."

Buttons were originally used for decoration. It wasn't until the 1300s that they were used as fasteners.

After buttons came zippers. The zipper was patented on August 29, 1893. Before it was called a zipper it was called a clasp locker. Zippers began to replace buttons on men's pants in the 1930s.

Next came Velcro. George de Mestral invented Velcro in the 1940s. The cockleburs that got stuck on his pants and in his dog's fur inspired him to create Velcro.

Instead of saying "button" or "zip" your lip, we could say, "Velcro your lip!"

Have you ever been awakened by the birds? They get up very early and can often be seen digging for worms. When your teacher says this to you, she is encouraging you to be early so that you don't miss out on anything.

Sometimes stores have sales called "early bird specials." Only the people that get to the store early, "the early birds," get the special deal. Look for "early bird specials" around the holidays.

This is a proverb that dates back to 1636. The Italians have a similar expression, *chi dorme, non piglia pesci*, which means, "He who sleeps catches no fish."

"The early bird gets the worm,"

my teacher likes to say.
I'm not sure what she means,
but I like it anyway.

If that's what you get when you're early,
then I guess I'd rather be late.
'Cuz an ooey, gooey, squishy worm
doesn't sound that great!

"I'm as hungry as a bear,"

my teacher likes to say.
I'm not sure what he means,
but I like it anyway.

When our teacher's really hungry,
he gets a beastly scowl.
But we know he's just a teddy bear
'cuz we've never heard him growl.

Your teacher is *really* hungry when he uses this expression because bears eat a lot. They eat an average of 35 pounds of food every day. It would take us two weeks to eat that much.

There are different kinds of bears that eat different kinds of foods. Grizzly bears eat berries, grass, fish, small animals like rats, and even bigger animals like deer. Polar bears eat fish and walruses, but their favorite dinner is seals. Pandas will eat bamboo for breakfast, lunch, and dinner. Sun bears really love honey and sloths like ants and termites.

We all know that teddy bears don't need food; they just need lots of love!

"Stick together!"

my teacher likes to say.
I'm not sure what she means,
but I like it anyway.

The duct tape didn't work
so we used some super glue.
And now we stick together
like our teacher told us to.

SUPER GLUE

Native
American
Celebration

NOVEMBER 1ST

Dinosaur
Discovery
Days

October 1ST

I loved going on field trips when I was a kid. Our teacher would say, "Stick together." It was fun to imagine all of us stuck together. What a mess!

When your teacher says, "Stick together," she wants you to stay close to one another so no one gets lost or left behind. But if you're silly like me, you can imagine whatever you want!

The first glue patent was issued in Britain in 1750. In 1951, Dr. Harry Coover discovered that cyanoacrylate, a sticky substance, was a useful product.

"The pen is mightier than the sword,"

my teacher likes to say.
I'm not sure what she means,
but I like it anyway.

I fought a monster in our room
as the class cheered and roared.
I won because I used my pen
and he only had his sword.

This expression began in 1582 as, "No more sword to be feared than the learned pen." It means that writing can be more powerful than fighting.

There have been many written documents that have been very powerful and prove how "mighty" written words can be. Consider the Declaration of Independence, the Magna Carta, and the Bible, to name a few.

"Every dog has its day,"

my teacher likes to say.
I'm not sure what he means,
but I like it anyway.

Today will be my dog's day.
He hasn't had his turn.
"How to be the teacher's pet"
the class is going to learn.

This expression was used by Shakespeare in *Hamlet* in act V, scene 1:

"Let Hercules himself do what he may,
The cat will mew, and the dog will have his day."

It means that eventually everyone will have an opportunity or get a chance at something.

Do you know what it means to be the "teacher's pet?"

If your dog had its day, what could he teach the class?

"These walls have ears,"

my teacher likes to say.
I'm not sure what she means,
but I like it anyway.

Some ears are BIG!
Some ears are small.
Who cleans the ears
that are on the wall?

This expression means to be careful of what you say because you never know who may be listening. It was used in World War II as a security slogan to warn people of enemy agents. It has been traced back to 1387 when it was, "Fields have eyes and woods have ears."

There are similar sayings in French, Spanish, German, and Russian.

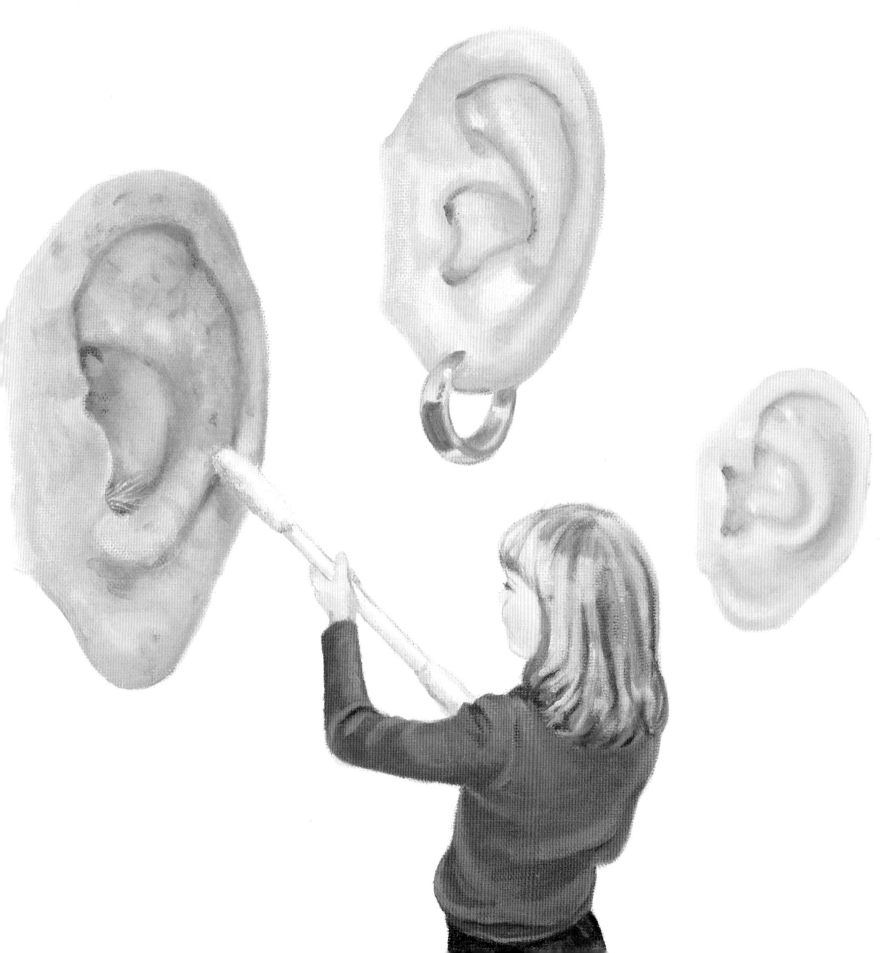

You may hear this expression said in different ways such as "Tall oaks from little acorns grow," or, "Little acorns into great oaks grow," but the meaning is the same: great things often start off very small.

When I was a kid my dad would say, "If your place in life seems small and unimportant just remember— the mighty oak was once a nut like you."

It first appeared in Chaucer's *Troilus and Criseyde*, written in 1385.

"Great oaks from little acorns grow,"
my teacher likes to say.
I'm not sure what she means,
but I like it anyway.

If a little tiny acorn
can become a giant tree,
then I can hardly wait
to see what I will be!

If you have ever watched monkeys you know that they can be very playful and silly. Your teacher may say this to you if you are fooling around and not getting your work done.

Can you think of other idioms that compare human behavior to animal behavior? (Hint: fox, owl, hen...)

"No more monkey business,"

my teacher likes to say.
I'm not sure what she means,
but I like it anyway.

We did what our teacher told us
and we hung the sign today.
We're going out of business,
so now we get to play!

Going
out of
business

Banana Smoothies
& Shakes $ 3.00

My teacher says so many things
that have a special way
of making me feel good inside
and brightening up my day.

So when she says, "I'll miss you,"
and, "I'm very proud of you,"
I really hope my teacher knows

I'm going to miss her too.

Denise Brennan-Nelson

Denise Brennan-Nelson's boundless energy and enthusiasm come from her days as a motivational speaker. Since the publication of her first book, *Buzzy the bumblebee* in 1999, Denise has taken that enthusiasm into schools and inspired thousands of children to "bee-lieve" in themselves. She is also the author of *My Momma Likes to Say*, a humorous look at the idioms and clichés mothers use, and *Penny: The Forgotten Coin*, which traces one penny's journey through history.

Denise lives in Howell, Michigan, with her husband, Bob, and their two daughters, Rebecca and Rachel.

Jane Monroe Donovan

Jane's first book, *Sunny Numbers: A Florida Counting Book*, led her to explore the flora and fauna of the Sunshine State. In her next book, *My Momma Likes to Say*, she was able to include the family dog, a yellow lab named Belle, and a Siamese cat named Maylee. For *My Teacher Likes to Say*, Jane was honored to feature her mother as the teacher throughout the book as well as her mother's third grade class as the students.

Jane lives in Pinckney, Michigan, with her husband, Bruce, and their two sons, Ryan and Joey, where she also raises and rides three horses: Ameera, Cherokee Rose, and Dozer.